The Path to ENLIGHTENMENT

The View of a Schizophrenic

DEVILISHLY ANGELIC

THE PATH TO ENLIGHTENMENT
THE VIEW OF A SCHIZOPHRENIC

iUniverse books may be ordered through booksellers or by contacting:

iUniverse
1663 Liberty Drive
Bloomington, IN 47403
www.iuniverse.com
1-800-Authors (1-800-288-4677)

ISBN: 978-1-5320-5263-7 (sc)
ISBN: 978-1-5320-5264-4 (e)

Library of Congress Control Number: 2018908133

Print information available on the last page.

iUniverse rev. date: 07/12/2018

To my children
without whom this book would have been
completed three years earlier.

In honor of my mother,
She was my light, my soul, and my motivation for greatness.

PREFACE

MOST LITERATURE ABOUT MENTAL HEALTH IS WRITTEN BY A THIRD party observing a client or patient. Feedback about medication side effects and withdrawal symptoms tends to come from self-reporting and observation.

I intend to provide an account of my experiences as a person who has received a diagnosis of schizophrenia. My hope is to inspire, motivate, and encourage young and old. Any obstacle can be overcome with the right motivation and dedication. I would like to open the eyes of mental health professionals and their clients to possibilities, and I hope to save a life through that process.

I hope I will inspire someone who has received a diagnosis of mental illness. We are not our diagnosis. We are people who suffer from symptoms. Everyone deserves a life, a choice, and a voice. I am proud to let the world see my perspective and experience my path to enlightenment.

ACKNOWLEDGMENTS

The completion of this book would not have been possible without the motivation and assistance of many people. Good and bad encounters have helped shape who I am today. We sometimes discredit the negative vibes or sour experiences. Learning from experiences and finding meaning in all situations help my mind and spirit to focus on a path to enlightenment.

PROBLEM RELATED TO LIFESTYLE

MANY DIFFERENT PERCEPTIONS HAVE CAUSED PEOPLE TO SPECULATE about what is and is not. I tried for years to figure out what was going on with me and why. When I was a small girl, I wondered about life and why I'd been dealt particular cards. I don't remember a lot about the struggle, but I do recall where I was.

I am the oldest of five children on my mother's side of the family. I was told I'm one of twenty-three children on my father's side. I have no evidence of this, but I have confirmed that my father had at least fifteen children. My mother was a lovely woman in my eyes, although she had her shortcomings just like anyone else. She had aspired to be a nurse, but life cut that dream short. My father was a man of the streets who made his millions, served time, and engaged in other activities typical of that lifestyle.

I lived the average life of a child who is a product of the Chicago ghetto. I grew up in the Chicago area which most people consider to be the *projects*, on the seventh floor of a high-rise. I recall always being afraid to look over the sides of that building because I had heard of people falling or being thrown out of the windows. I was a little girl, maybe around four years old, when we moved there. One of the first things my stepfather did was to put up the bunk beds. My mother was not a television watcher, and I remember sitting on my bed and listening to music playing on the radio. We heard songs such as Keith Sweat's "Make It Last Forever," Johnny Gill's "My, My, My," and others from that era. I particularly loved the Isley Brothers. Soul was the favorite genre of music in my family.

My stepfather appeared when I was a few months old, and for a long time I believed that he was my father. He never treated me any different from his two daughters, including me in all family functions and always introducing me as his daughter when we were out. His family never intruded or tried to tell me otherwise, and even today they still refer to me as family. We had everything we needed, as I recall, and life was grand. My stepfather had three daughters with my mother, and I remember hearing them talk about marriage and spending the rest of their lives together.

I don't recall the specific details, but eventually my stepfather left. After a few months, I came to understand that he had gone to jail for stealing. I got letters in the mail from him with beautiful drawings on the envelopes, and I always wondered about those drawings. My uncle was in jail around that same time, though in a different location, and they both had the same type of art on their envelopes. I never asked about it, but I assume those envelopes were printed that way and the inmates just gave the drawings their own spin. Who knows? Maybe someday I'll figure it out, but right now it's not important.

I was staying at my aunt and uncle's house on Stony Island when I first met my mother's new boyfriend, who wore military clothing. Eavesdropping on my mother's conversation with my aunt, I heard her say he was a veteran who had killed people—even children— during the war because he had been ordered to do so. But I didn't really pay too much attention to this new person. As a child, I was a free spirit who didn't care about adult matters.

I loved nature and always wanted to be outside in the elements. Rather than playing with others all the time, I preferred being alone and exploring what the world had to offer. Don't get me wrong—I was able to socialize with others when I needed to, but I easily got irritated with other people. I spent my time wondering about the world, whereas others focused on materialistic things and the opposite sex. I wasn't into boys—I just wanted to enjoy the moment and leave it at that.

After a few months, the new man moved in with us, but I don't recall having much interaction with him at first. For the most part, he ignored me and my sisters. He did things such as cooking for us and taking us to the park, but I don't remember spending any personal, interactive moments together. He was a high-spirited person who drank a little too much, in my opinion at that time. I didn't like people who were different from my mother, who didn't smoke, drink, or go out much.

My mother enjoyed reading good books and spending quality time with family. Sometimes I would hear her sister and brothers making fun of her and trying to get her to drink, but she wouldn't drink any kind of alcoholic beverage, not even a wine cooler. Instead, she'd take out a pot and make some iced tea. I did not like the fact that her boyfriend smoked and drank. Every time he asked me to get him a beer out of the refrigerator, I would shake it up. Thinking back, I don't know why he kept asking me to get his beer for him, because he knew I would shake it up every time. Every now and then I would hear my mother tell me that I'd better not shake up his can, but I would do it anyway.

One day I woke up to my mother crying hysterically. At the time, I didn't know why she was crying, but it went on for days. She would sit in her room and cry her eyes out. Later she announced she was pregnant with my little brother. When he was born, she told people he was born with sickle cell, but he later grew out of it. I do recall his dad, the army guy, having sickle cell because I witnessed a few of his seizures.

When I started kindergarten, my mother took me to school and walked me to my classroom for the first couple of days. The next week, she walked me to the playground, but while I was playing,

I looked around and couldn't find her. I ran around crying and screaming hysterically for my mother. I recall being very cold and bending down to cover my legs with my skirt to stay warm. When the bell rang for us to get in line and walk back into the school building, I kept crying and looking for my mother. Eventually a woman from the school took my hand and walked me to my class.

That lady stayed with me the whole day because I was still in "zombie mode." I wouldn't speak or do any work, because in my mind I had been abandoned and the school had kidnapped me. Oh, how I feared that I would never see my family again. Then I heard someone yell, "Whose mother?" I looked up and there she was, in all her glory, to pick me up from school. You would have thought I had won a big bag of candy and chips. (Kindergarten mind, right? LOL.)

BRAIN WAVES OF THOUGHT

I named this chapter "Problem Related to Lifestyle" because the story is typical of what a person talks about on their first visit with a therapist. The therapist uses the first few sessions to explore their client's thoughts, strengths, and weaknesses. Depending on what form of therapy is being used, the therapist might also explore historical events.

Looking back, I realize how that moment was important, because it helped shape the person I have become and the abandonment issues with which I have struggled over the years. Being left unattended without any warning or explanation can be traumatic for a young child. I went off to play, unaware that I had been left alone. That might not have been such an important event for some children, but I felt betrayed and developed abandonment issues. As I think about the relationship I had with my mother, I realize that she was, in effect, my God.

Over the years, I have continued to look back, especially at the lack of communication between parent and child. I wouldn't have felt abandoned if my mother had made me aware that she would be leaving, assured me that everything would be okay, and directed me to an adult in case I need assistance. Sometimes we don't go through this kind of process because we don't have time, or we impulsively do things without thinking about the consequences. Working mothers and fathers have busy schedules and might not think about making sure their child feels secure about attending day care or school.

The signs that we can look for in our children include excessive emotional distress and repeated complaints. For example, a child might repeatedly ask their parent to stay, or they might engage in regressive behaviors. They could develop separation anxiety and display a persistent fear of being alone and excessive requests for reassurance of safety.

Although this is not an inclusive list of possibilities, I wanted to shed light on one important developmental concern as experienced by me and possibly by others. At times we overlook the small details of children's thought processes because we are consumed with our own concerns, such as depression or anxiety.

This line of thought could be expanded, of course, but my intent is simply to focus on a single perspective, a pivotal moment that shaped my own parenting style. I want to emphasize that I do not mean to judge other people or argue that my way is the right way. Please read these brain waves of thoughts as they are presented—as my perspective on my own life and how I have processed, explored, and confirmed it. Any single event may or may not have contributed to my diagnosis or mental health status. In therapy, we can only evaluate the case and make our best clinical judgment of the cause, depending on our conceptualization of human development.

CHILDHOOD TRAUMA AND PSYCHOSIS

The Lord guided them by a pillar of cloud during
the day and a pillar of fire at night.
—Exodus 13:21, New Living Translation

EVERY NIGHT MY MOTHER WOULD TURN ON THE RADIO AND LISTEN
to oldies all night. This happened so regularly that even now as an
adult, I can turn on the radio, listen to oldies, and fall right to sleep.
In fact, for a long time I wasn't able to fall asleep unless I had the
radio on. I eventually had to break that habit, but that is a story I
would talk about later.

My mother didn't like lights being on if they weren't being
used, especially at night. She went out and bought night-lights for
every room, so we wouldn't be in the dark. Those night–lights were
pivotal points for me, because they started my quest for the meaning
of life. My night–light, which was an ivory color, was a figure of the
Virgin Mary with her hands together as if she were praying. It was
a typical Catholic figure that anyone would picture when thinking
of the Virgin Mary.

My family is Catholic, and my grandmother taught us how to pray and honor our parents. I didn't read the Bible when I was young, but my grandmother would tell us the classic stories of biblical characters such as Noah, Jesus, and Moses. We didn't learn about other things in the Bible—just intricate details about these people. Neither did we go to church or worship in any way in my mother's house.

One night when I was eight or nine years old, I woke up in the middle of the night needing to go to the bathroom. But first I lay in bed, on the bottom bunk and facing the wall, for a little while to collect myself. As I turned over to face the door, for some reason I glanced at the night-light on the wall directly in front of me. I stared at that Virgin Mary night-light, looking closely at its details. After a few minutes, I looked toward the door and tried to find the courage to get up.

Just as I started to get up, I glanced at the upper left corner of the door and noticed a cloud moving from one side of the door to the other. The cloud was fluorescent and the same ivory color as the Virgin Mary night-light. Moving from left to right, it gradually covered the top of the door. It was as if I was standing outside and watching a cloud move across the sky. Then it started to move down toward the floor, and it appeared to be forming into the shape of a human body. Before it completed itself, I closed my eyes and tried to scream, but I couldn't make a sound. All I could do was close my eyes.

When I opened my eyes, the cloud was gone. I ran to my mother's room and told her that I had a bad headache, so that she would give me some attention. I didn't want to tell her what had happened, because her new boyfriend was in the room. He looked like he wanted to send me away regardless of what I was going to say.

I often felt like I was in the way when he was around, and I was never comfortable talking to my mother when he was in the room. I don't know what gave me that feeling, because he never did anything to cause it. He never laid a hand on me or my other siblings, nor did I ever hear him speak ill of us. That night, he was the one who got up and took me back to my room. Then he gave me a Tylenol and made sure I was okay before he left the room to go back to bed.

Sometime when things like that happen, we tell ourselves that it was just a dream. I really wish that had been a dream. After that first incident, it didn't matter whose house I was at or what time of day it was. Any time I was struggling to go to sleep, that cloud would appear in the doorway. After that first time, it stayed at the top of the door and didn't start to form a shape—and after a few minutes, I would fall asleep. Eventually I began thinking of it as a positive entity, because when it appeared, I would relax rather than feel frightened.

After that first experience, I started to hear and see things more often. I would hear my name being called directly in my ear—sometimes subtly, but at other times loudly as if someone were yelling at me. Sometimes I would wake up after hearing my name called, but nobody would be there. It seemed to happen randomly, and I never knew when to expect it. When I started to ignore the voices, however, they eventually stopped.

I have reason to believe that entity needed to get my attention, though. One afternoon not long afterward, I was playing hide-and-seek with my siblings. Back then, cartoon character slippers were popular among kids, and my mother had bought me a pair of yellow slippers with Tweety bird's head on the front. Well, I ran into my room and hid in the closet where, of course, all our shoes and clothes were. While waiting for someone to find me, and for no particular reason, I looked down at one of those slippers. I was just waiting … looking at the slipper, then at something else … looking at the slipper, then at something else.

Suddenly that Tweety bird's eyes shifted and looked directly at me—*directly at me*! I ran out of the closet, though it felt like I was moving in slow motion. The room seemed to spin and fade out, as though I were about to die. I remember it like it was yesterday, and I had never in my life felt so afraid. Right in front of me I watched those eyes slowly move, from looking away to looking directly at me. Can you imagine? What would you have done? I was only about ten years old.

I ran and told my mother what had happened, but I don't remember her response. Maybe my fear was so profound that it blocked my memory of what she said or did. As you might expect, I threw those slippers away. Ever since then, I have been seeing objects move in front of me—not drastically, but just slightly. Sometimes I see something move just half an inch or roll a short distance, so subtly that if I hadn't seen it move with my own eyes, I wouldn't notice it.

I don't recall exact dates and times, but rather events and how I felt at the time. My mother would play the oldies on the radio every night to calm the house. One night I fell asleep, but then something woke me up. I remember lying on my back and opening my eyes. As I started to turn over, I happened to glance down toward the foot of the bed. The room was dark except for a faint light coming from the bathroom, where my mother kept a light on at night just in case. I saw a black figure in the shape of a grown man, from the waist up, lying across the foot of my bed. It looked as if the figure was sitting on the floor, with only his upper body stretched across the bottom of the bed. His head was resting on my bed as though looking away, but *his arm was reaching toward me as if to touch or grab me!*

I stared at this figure for hours, but it never moved. It was like it had intentionally frozen, thinking I wouldn't see it if it didn't move. I didn't take my eyes off it, but it didn't move, breathe, or disappear ... Eventually I couldn't fight my sleepiness, and I drifted off. When I woke up, the black figure was gone. I don't remember what I was feeling. I just remember that I didn't move, yell for help, or attempt to kick it to see what it was. I don't remember mentioning anything to my mother. I just proceeded with my day and went to school.

Weeks went by, and I was on my way home from school. I decided to take the stairs, rather than the elevator, up to the seventh floor. I don't remember why, although sometimes there were so many people waiting for the elevator that taking the stairs was quicker. I was skipping up the stairs by myself and suddenly ...

Bump! I was snatched up by a man who proceeded to drag me down the stairs. Nobody helped me. Wasn't I screaming? Didn't anyone see me fighting him to let me go? The guy managed to get me out of the building, but just then—to my surprise—my uncle was walking *into* the building. Just in time! My uncle grabbed me away from the stranger and told me to go upstairs. I never saw that man again. I don't know what happened to him, nor will I disclose my uncle's name—just in case something *did* happen to him. This is the first time I've really thought about what happened. I recall my mother and uncle talking about it back then, but to be honest I just went in the house like nothing had happened. I never spoke about that incident to my mother or anyone else.

Wow! As I write about the incident now, I wonder why I wasn't more concerned. Why did I just act like nothing had happened? Why didn't my mom ask me anything? I know that she was aware of what had happened, because I heard my uncle tell her what he had seen. I don't remember their whole conversation because I didn't care enough to pay attention. Even now I don't feel anything but emptiness, although I find it interesting that I feel no emotion when I think about what happened. It's something to think about later, but honestly I might never think about it again after I finish writing this paragraph.

BRAIN WAVE OF THOUGHT

Childhood trauma and psychosis is the main focus of this chapter. According to John Read (2014), more than 125 research studies have supported the theory that early childhood trauma can affect brain development in children in later life. A clinical therapist might assume that a client has suffered some physical or sexual abuse, emphasizing night terrors, perhaps.

I might have forgotten to mention that I grew up with a loving mother, although her nurturing skills may not have been the best. I knew my mother loved me and attended to my well-being, but

I have yearned for emotional support. In my earliest memory of attempting to give my mother a hug, she quickly pushed me away. I don't recall her directly telling me that she loved me, although I heard her say it to her partner. I also heard her tell other people how much she loved her children. Typically, the behavioral condition that might best describe my childhood trauma may include, but not be limited to, childhood emotional neglect because of a mother who was too busy to fully nurture.

As a child, I would theorize, I may have suffered from some dissociated phenomenon as a maladaptive coping mechanism resulting from emotional pain (the white cloud that comforted me at night). Although I eagerly thirsted for comfort and security at night, I never discussed that with my mother. Deep down I wanted her to read me a fairy tale and then kiss me on the forehead. I always wanted to run to my mother for comfort, but her partners got in the way. (That's my inner child thinking.) Maybe I felt like they were stealing her from me. Maybe I had some Freudian childhood thinking, but with my mother.

Because my emotional needs were not met, the eventual result was psychosis. Clinicians sometimes discredit the effects of emotional neglect, but I didn't know how to process my thoughts, feelings, or emotions. I was just told either to sit somewhere or go play. Children's needs should be validated. As a child, when I wanted to cry, nobody comforted me, so where did those emotions go? I always felt alone and vulnerable, without any sense of emotional security from my family. My paranoia about being alone and vulnerable overwhelmed me, and I began to create unrealistic schemas to confirm and validate my feelings of being alone.

All I wanted was to be validated—to hear someone say that I was loved and secure, to feel a hug, kiss, or any physical affection. I wanted to be able to process my emotions—to know what a normal emotion is and what to do with it. Without guidance, children cannot process emotions on their own and enjoy positive emotional development. Looking back at my childhood psychosis, I hypothesize that I was simply validating my fears and paranoia by creating unrealistic—yet real—hallucinations to help me feel normal. Over time, as I began to develop relationships, physical affection became abnormal, but we will discuss this phenomena later.

Let's not forget about the traumatic event of being left at school.

POST-TRAUMATIC STRESS DISORDER

LIVING IN THE HIGH-RISE WAS NOT AN UNPLEASANT EXPERIENCE. MY personal, in-home experiences were what made things interesting. I recall witnessing domestic violence at home—waking up several times to my mom fighting with my brother's father and hearing that he stole Mom's money for drugs. Once when I was taking a nap in my mother's room, I awoke to see her wrestling my brother's father on the floor. I sat up and watched them struggle. She was trying to get her purse back from him, but he eventually got the upper hand and ran out the front door. I don't recall what happened next, but I probably just went back to sleep. Why? Why did my experiences seem normal?

I recall several incidents of my brother's father stealing from the household. One day my mom told him to leave, so he walked out the front door—but he didn't leave. He just sat on a crate outside the door and kept asking my mother to let him back in. The weather was nice, and as I looked out the window at him, several kids were outside playing on the porch. When I noticed him slitting his wrist with a sharp object, I called for my mother and told her he was bleeding. She called an ambulance and held his wrist until the medics arrived and took him to the hospital. She had been going to school for nursing, so I believe she knew what she was doing. There was blood all over the porch, so my mom then took a bucket of water and bleach and mopped it up.

After a few days, my mother took him back. I later witnessed several more occasions of fighting and arguments between them, but I wasn't bothered too much by it. I was just too engrossed in my own world of seeing things to be concerned.

As time went by, our family grew and we moved to the Parkways Garden apartments. We were excited. From my perspective as a child, we were moving on up. We were not in the high-rise anymore, although we were just across the street from it. The apartment was cute, and the best part was that, having lived on the seventh floor in the high-rise, we were now just on the fourth floor.

At a young age, I was not very good at sharing what I was thinking with the world. At times, my mother would keep us close and not let us play outside with other children. We were always restricted to certain areas and told, "Don't go past the gate" or "Stay on this floor." There was something called "the rink" that was popular at the time. The last time I was in Chicago, it had been turned into a church, but when I was a kid, everyone I knew would go there to skate and dance. Every week, my friends and I asked my mother if I could go to the rink, but she always said no. Even when allowed to attend certain functions or events, my siblings and I weren't permitted to go too far. We spent most of our time sitting silently while watching other kids play. This wasn't always the case, but it was more often than not.

I will never understand why my mother was so protective. She took care of us and never pushed us away as if she didn't want us around. In fact, it was more like she always held us on her hip, as though she was afraid to lose us. Could it have been because we were in the heart of Chicago, where almost every day we heard gunshots? Who knows? At this point I can only speculate or hypothesize.

We had some challenging times, and the Department of Child and Family Services (DCFS) sometimes got involved. I wouldn't say my mother was abusive, and as I recall, I earned my spankings. But from time to time we got spankings that left marks on us. It was rare for my mother to hit us, but when she did, it was fierce. The first time DCFS was involved, my grandmother had called them after asking some questions of my siblings and me. DCFS showed up, took pictures of our bruises, and then left us with our grandmother for a while. Fortunately, my mother didn't take that situation lightly. She made sure that she followed all the necessary protocols—classes and so on—to get us back, and my father showed up to assist with money. Later in life, I heard that my grandmother had not been concerned with our well-being, but that her motive had been to get a welfare check. My mother had five children, which at that time probably meant a lot of food stamps and cash for us all. I don't know if that accusation is true or not, and I don't care enough to find out. I never talked to either my mother or my grandmother about it.

Several times DCFS was called because of problems such as a lack of food in our home, but my mother would always figure out how to keep us and move on. I have always been a mother's girl, so those times when we were separated were agonizing. I recall feeling anxious and crying if I was away from her too long, and I'd get frightened when I overheard other people talk about how they could keep my siblings and me. Looking back, I now realize that those people either weren't aware of my presence or just didn't care about not discussing certain topics around me.

I personally believe most accusations came from greed. Several family members would make comments about how much government assistance they would receive if they got us. Sometimes you must sit back and think about what people say around you and take it seriously. I think about that when I see people at funerals and weddings. People talk about how good a person was, when they were just trying to make money off you. Back then I never heard anyone talking about our poor living conditions. Instead, every conversation was about how much government money my mom received because she had five children.

It's sad to have a family that focuses on monetary gain rather than on helping each other. I'm not saying that every encounter with my family was bad, but certain conversations just shouldn't happen, especially in front of children. Families need to do a better job of demonstrating unity and security. I always felt insecure about talking to some family members because of what I overheard from others— talking about each other, or intentionally causing problems. I learned early not to trust people. How could I? How can I trust people when my own family members create such unnecessary drama?

I grew up hearing how certain family members would sleep with each other's boyfriends, husbands, girlfriends, and wives. I grew up hearing about cousins having children by each other. Several conversations about incest hit my ear, and I heard how someone had stolen from someone else. I heard family members criticizing others who were going through hard times. My family is resourceful, yet some people would rather watch others struggle than step in and help them. I will never understand this mentality. How can anyone allow their own flesh and blood to suffer when they are more than capable of assisting?

My brother is also my cousin—we share a father, but my aunt is his mother. I am the oldest, so it doesn't affect me as much, and my mother was done with my father long before it happened. Often I wonder what my brother thinks about his situation, but that's not my burden to carry. That's something my father and aunt have to live with. I still speak to my brother, though I have yet to explain the situation to my children—and I might never do so.

For a long time, I lived at my grandmother's house, although I don't recall why or how we ended up there. When I would ask to call my mother, they'd tell me she wasn't home. Several weeks went by, and I'd occasionally overhear my grandmother talking to someone about my mother being in the hospital. When they'd ask her why, my grandmother would make a symbol with her hands but I've never known what that symbol meant. That was the first time we stayed away from my mother for so long without speaking to her or her visiting to check on us.

My mother was still in a relationship with the army guy, who had begun to act weird. I woke a few times to them fighting, and she was often trying to stop him from stealing from us. Once I woke to find her rolling around on the floor, wrestling him to try to get her purse away from him. I never will understand why she continued to let him back in the house. The cycle never ended. He would be gone for a little while, and then I would see him back in the house and stealing from us again.

Once he was gone for a few months, and when he resurfaced, he looked different. When I got home from school, he was watching *The Simpsons*. Although we never had much interaction, we did watch cartoons together occasionally, but that time he started talking with me about the world in general. I had never paid too much attention to him, but he had definitely changed. He had lost weight, and I could see deep pockets in his skin as if it were sinking in. He was coughing badly and acting like it hurt him to move. There was a bucket on the side of the bed for him to throw up in. I could tell that he was very sick, but I didn't know what he was suffering from.

Not too long after that, my mother told us that he had passed away in the nursing home. I overheard that he was stiff and dehydrated when they found him, and that they had to break some bones to get him dressed for his funeral. My mom wore the ring that he had given her. They had planned to get married, but unfortunately things never made it to that point. I felt sad to be at his funeral, but I tried hard to hide my emotions by pretending to be asleep or doing things to distract myself. I never liked seeing my mother cry or be in pain, so I always felt the need to remove myself to avoid it. One day perhaps I will explore this, but I can't make any promises.

Over the years, I noticed that my mother was changing. In my memory, she was a beautiful woman who kept her hair done and was always dressed pretty. She would hire a babysitter so that she could go out with her family on weekends. But gradually I noticed that her hair was falling out and there were nasty sores on her scalp.

She would lose a lot of weight, but then gain it all back. She told us that she had walking pneumonia, and I never questioned her even though it scared me. Sometimes she would be in the hospital for a long time, but I wouldn't call anyone to let them know we were in the house by ourselves. I would go out and steal food and money so that we could survive until she got home, and several times we didn't have heat or hot water. I would cook for us and make sure we were okay, but I never told anyone. I lied to my siblings and other people about where my mother was. When my uncle would come over, I'd tell him that my mother was working a double shift or a night shift. I feared separation from my mother, and I hated being away from her during the times of DCFS.

I had several boyfriends during that time, and I would go and take a shower at their home. But I had little interest in boys and no interest in sex; in fact, I preferred to be with the same sex. Looking back, I think I was too occupied with keeping my family together. I didn't want to talk to many people because I was afraid that my situation would show and they would ask questions, although I wasn't ashamed of my circumstances. I've never talked with my siblings to see what they remember.

There were times when I was scared to go to sleep, although I don't know why. I preferred to sleep in my mother's room, so I would sneak in there and lie across her legs. She'd often have a throw-up bucket next to her bed. I always knew something was going on, but I coped by pushing it to the back of my mind. I would cry at night for my mother, because I was always afraid of losing her.

When I was a kid, she'd tell my siblings and me that we got on her nerves, and several times she threatened to take the youngest child and leave the rest of us. Now I know she was saying that out of frustration, but for a long time I believed her—and it hurt. It hurt my soul, especially since I was a mother's girl. I would sit in a corner and wish to die when she said things like that, because I saw no need for my existence. When I'd run up to my mother for a hug, she would push me away. Nevertheless, I still had faith in my relationship with my mother.

One of my mother's childhood sweethearts would appear every so often over the years to see her. He would write to me, though, and tell me that he was coming only to see me. He told me that if he could, he would leave with me and we would be together. I never understood this when I was a child, and I didn't tell my mother because she seemed so happy when he was around. He made several uncomfortable advances toward me over the years, but I would just dismiss them. I told myself that as long he didn't touch me, I was okay.

One day when I was in ninth grade, he called my mother and asked her to send me to his house. I don't recall his reason, but I went to his house after school and we sat outside and talked about how my day was going. When he asked if I would help him get something out of his basement, I said sure and proceeded to follow him into the house. Going down the stairs, however, he turned around and tried to kiss me. When I pushed him back and said, "What the hell?" he stood there as if surprised at my reaction. I turned around, left his house, and went home, having lost all respect for that man. I saw him several times after that, but he was always careful about what he said and did around me. He knew that I didn't tell my mother, and I never shared what had happened with anyone else.

BRAIN WAVE OF THOUGHT

There are several circumstances mentioned in this chapter that could cause traumatic stress. Let's examine some clinical behavioral definitions of post-traumatic stress disorder (PTSD). Evidently I was exposed to threats of death or significant injury that resulted in an intense emotional response of hopelessness. As a child, watching someone attempt suicide was interesting. I experienced disturbances later in life, once I understood what was going on in front of me. Immediate counseling might have closed my case out successfully, but counselors were not trained properly. Children may not develop a traumatic response right away, especially if they don't know the consequences or dynamics of an event. When I fully understood suicide, my mind moved this memory to my subconscious. Only then did I start to really feel or experience traumatic symptoms.

Clinicians should not discredit the conversation or avoid explaining. I would have liked for my mother or a counselor to have processed and explained what was going on around me and provided me with some security and safety. Instead, my experiences were treated as normal phenomena, and maladaptive behaviors and stressful circumstances were not explained to me so that I could process them. I was left alone to process emotions that I did not understand, which resulted in an inability to experience a normal full range of emotions, including love, as an adult.

Although I had a child's understanding, I knew that what was going on around me was not right. My understanding of love was diminished. I was not able to grasp the reasons why the concept of love would cause so much distress, so I gradually decided that I didn't want that emotion or faulty thinking. Because I was numb and unable to connect emotionally, several of my adult friendships and intimate relationships failed. I can still recall several conversations in which I was accused of being coldhearted because I couldn't relate or respond to emotional cues.

Detaching from other people and avoiding emotional thoughts and feelings became my strategy for avoiding heartache from relationships. Whenever I felt like I wanted to love someone and be close to them, I went into flight mode. I unconsciously sabotaged my relationships by acting like I didn't care or avoiding the situation altogether. For example, I would avoid answering my phone and decline invitations to events. I developed a fear of people getting too close, because I worried that I wouldn't know how to recognize or be able to terminate an unhealthy relationship. I was scared of getting caught in the same cycle that my mother experienced.

Clinicians should help their clients develop and implement coping skills that will help them normalize their feelings and emotions, so that they can engage in relationships and social activities without fear of rejection. It took me years to recognize that I was in need of coping skills, and it took even longer to realize that I needed to value relationships. Sometimes we may be afraid to be vulnerable, especially after we've lived for years on a lonely island.

The fear of change and rejection can be difficult to manage, but the key is to develop self-worth. When you know your own worth, rejection doesn't hurt as much. Then the process of change can be seen as a path to enlightenment. Motivate yourself with the well-known motto that applies to all forms of personal training: "Without the pain there will be no gain."

RELIGIOUS OR SPIRITUAL PROBLEM

ONE NIGHT IN MY EARLY TEEN YEARS—I CAN'T REMEMBER MY EXACT age—I had an interesting dream about meeting God. The dream started with me trying to save myself from drowning by swimming up to the surface of a large body of water, where I found debris floating around. Managing to climb on top of some debris, I looked around to assess the situation and saw that it was a flood. I appeared to be right in the middle of a catastrophe. Everything was gone and there was just water everywhere. Buildings had been destroyed, and I saw a few dead bodies floating around me. Then someone else on a floating device came close to me and reached for my hand, and instantly it was like I was in another place. That individual was still with me—although I can't tell you for sure if it was human, partly because I don't recall looking directly at it. It just stayed right beside me, yet maybe one step behind.

Then I found myself climbing up a cliff. When I reached the top, I was able to look down on great portions of the earth. I could see cities and zoom in on specific areas. One area caught my eye—a city built completely of metal. There was silver everywhere, in the buildings and roads, and right in the middle of the city was a huge eye. It was looking around and observing everything. Eventually it looked at me on the cliff, and instantly I found myself in another place.

This time I found myself standing in a hallway lined with doors. Everything was white, as if I were inside a cloud. There were no defined lines or symmetry, but I could tell it was a hallway. The same entity was next to me, and although I don't recall hearing words come from its mouth, I felt its directions. Just as before, it didn't move in front of me or come within my eyesight, but I had a gut feeling about what to do. Was the entity speaking to my soul? I know it may not make sense, and I might not be describing the experience very well. I just know that although I didn't hear the entity with my ears, I definitely heard it nonetheless. We eventually came to a door and I was instructed to walk inside. When I did so, a powerful sensation came over me. The room was white, but not like the white that we know. I have yet to see that color on earth, so I can't describe to you a point of reference.

In front of me was God. I cannot describe to you what it was, how it looked, or how big it was. It was more of a feeling. I stood in that room, and God told me the purpose of my life. It felt like I was in that room for hours, receiving detailed instructions. Then, just like that, I woke up. I felt amazing, a feeling I have yet to feel on this earth again. You might be wondering what I was told to do. Honestly, I do not know. I woke up not remembering anything that I had been told.

For years, I've looked back on that day and wondered. Why would I be given a master plan, yet wake up remembering nothing? I recall having the conversation and hearing the words, but my mind retained only the visual—not the audio. Should I attempt hypnotism to try to remember the words? I thought about it, but I feel that everything happens for a reason, so I don't want to interfere with design.

Years later I was at a time in my life when I wanted to find answers, so I considered various religions. My family is Catholic, and we lived next to a huge Catholic church when I was a teenager. I attended that church every Sunday for a month, but it didn't capture my attention or answer any of my questions. In fact, Catholicism simply raised more questions for me, such as Why should we worship the woman who gave birth to Jesus? Why was she so important? The first commandment says that our God is a jealous God, and that we shouldn't put anything or anyone before him. If that's the case, then why am I sitting here and praising this statue, as if I don't know how to follow directions? Also, the Bible says that Jesus came not to change the law, but to enforce it. Yet he began his prayer by saying, "Our father, who art in heaven." So why do we pray to Jesus and say "in Jesus's name" at the end of our prayers? I hear a lot of people pray to Jesus and claim that other scriptures tell them to do this. But if God gave us the Ten Commandments and Jesus himself told us to do things in such a manner, then why do something different?

I believe that Jesus was sent as a role model to show us how to live, not as someone whom we should worship. We are all children of God, according to the Bible. Now here is the confusing part—I also don't believe in the stories of the Bible. I have read about and practiced several religions: Buddhism; Christianity, including Catholicism; Wicca; and Satanism, to name a few. Actually the only reason I ventured into Christianity was that my first husband was a Christian and we got baptized together. I believed at that time that I should follow my husband's lead in religion, partly because I believed in the unity and happiness of marriage.

I don't claim or practice any specific religion. Instead, I believe that all religions have some truth in them, so I took from several and created my own belief system. I believe there is a higher power and that I have met it, so I can't deny its existence. I belief in unity, peace, and the righteousness of everyone. In my life, I also apply *The Secret*, a movie based on a book created to explain the law of attraction. Since introduced to this concept, I have applied it to my life, along with other beliefs, and I believe it has worked for me.

I strongly believe in the spirit world, partly because I have had too many encounters with the spirit world to deny it. A lot of people

THE PATH TO ENLIGHTENMENT

would say this is because of my diagnosis of schizophrenia, but I guess it depends on how you look at it. In some cultures, I would not be considered a person who needs a lot of medication. I have read that some people view schizophrenia as a gift, a higher state of consciousness or enlightenment. I once heard that after Adam and Eve were kicked out of the Garden of Eden, they kept trying to get back in. God moved them away over and over again, and eventually he put other entities in front of Eden to guard it. At some point, God put a veil over humans so that they couldn't see the Garden of Eden and the spirit world. As I said earlier, I don't believe everything I hear, but I do believe there is some truth in everything.

I believe several people have been gifted with the ability to connect with the spirit world, yet they're afraid to use their gift because it runs counter to cultural norms. With all the challenges you face in life, the harder you fight destiny, the harder it is to get on track. The movie *Final Destination* is about a man who foresees a major disaster in which several people will die, so he changes circumstances to save their lives. In the movie, destiny finds ways to catch up with those people and kill them anyway but in a more gruesome way. This movie is a perfect example of what I mean by destiny and faith. You can't escape your destiny, because it will eventually find you.

I have been contacted by the spirit world several times, sometimes by seeing faces on the wall or ceiling. One day in 2014, when I was in the navy and stationed in San Antonio, I was in my apartment waiting for my husband to get home. At that time I had only one child, a two-year-old boy. Sitting in the front room watching television, I glanced to my right and saw a face on the wall by the door. The face never went away. When my husband got home and saw the face, he thought maybe the paint had just dried that way. We had recently moved into that apartment, which had been newly painted.

Several months went by, and the face didn't go away—but it never moved either, so I tried to put it out of my mind. I rarely sat in the front room of my apartment; even now I spend most of my time in my bedroom. One day, just as before, I was sitting in our front room and waiting for my husband to get home. When I picked up my phone to call him, a ghostly female figure appeared on the left side of my screen. She opened her mouth unnaturally wide, like in the movies, as if her lower jaw just dropped straight down. I don't know if she was trying to talk to me or perhaps to scream, because I didn't give her a chance. I dropped the phone and ran toward the door.

As I ran, I glanced at the face on the wall by the door, and it appeared to move slightly as if coming off the wall. I tried to run faster, but it felt as though I were running in slow motion. The room seemed to elongate, so that I felt farther and farther from the door, and then it started moving slightly from right to left. It seemed like an eternity before I finally got out the door, and by then my anxiety was so high that I almost collapsed. Then I looked back and saw my son coming behind me—with the phone! I screamed for him to stop and put the phone down, but not because I was afraid for him. I had concluded years earlier that whatever was going on wanted only *my* attention and that therefore the people around me weren't in any danger. Then I sat in my car waiting for my husband, a wonderful man, to get home from work. I didn't want to go back into the house that night, so he sat with me in the car until morning.

While I was in the navy, several other similar situations occurred, and eventually I was admitted to the hospital for the first time. That started a chain of events that pushed my symptoms out of control and threatened my sanity. I won't explain those events, since they happened while I was still in the military and I don't want to get a letter from the government. I really don't know what might happen, but since I'm unsure, I'd rather not touch on it.

I will never understand how people's problems are diagnosed or why they are prescribed medication. I have been admitted to several inpatient hospitals, and one thing I learned in my years of "freaking out" is that medication doesn't work. On several occasions when I was admitted, I took the prescribed medications *only* because I was told that if I didn't, I would never get out. What a terrible thing to say to someone. I was supposed to be there to get help, but I was treated like a criminal. It never failed. At every hospital to which I was admitted, I was forced to take meds and I received no real therapy.

The only times anyone talked to me were during the intake process when I was first admitted, and then when I was released, to explain the medications with which I was sent home. While I was in the hospital, I would see a psychologist only once—for ten minutes. As a licensed therapist with certifications in other therapy specialties, I now know this was a horrible method and an injustice to the mental health community. How could any psychologist accurately treat me—or help me at all—based on only ten minutes of conversation? The only thing we ever talked about was how I was feeling at the time. Literally every time I was admitted, that was the gist of those conversations.

Usually I would refuse to take the medications because of the side effects, but at one point I *did* take the medication in hopes that it would work. It made me sleepy, so I went to my room to take a nap. While I was lying there on my bed, I started feeling paranoid. I got a strong feeling that something was in my room.

When that happens, I see things in my mind that I can't actually see with my eyes, almost like a sixth sense. That may not make sense, but it's true. In those moments, I know that other people can't see what I am seeing. It's similar to experiencing a daydream, during which you "see" a mental picture of something that nobody else can see. When I see things in my mind, I am fully conscious in the moment, but I'm using some sense other than my vision. Sometimes I see something that doesn't realize that I'm aware of its presence. Some entities don't mess with me—they just go around doing whatever they want to do—but others obviously want me to notice them.

On that occasion in the hospital, I was lying on my bed when I saw something in my room. I was afraid and wanted to run out of the room, but I couldn't move, because I was highly sedated from the medication. When I tried to get up, I was too drowsy to move, even though I was fully aware of what I was seeing. I wasn't actually asleep, but my body felt heavy. I have never felt so much fear in my life. Just imagine wanting to run from danger but being unable to move. I talked to the nurse about it later, and she said the my inability to move was a side effect of the medication.

After that incident, I vowed to never again take medication. That didn't stop my symptoms, but it *did* stop my paranoia and impulse to run. Why would society do this to someone? Why has nobody else talked about their experience on that medication? Are they scared that if they speak up, they'll just be given more medication and the horrible treatment won't end?

Also, hospital food was unbearable. Do hospitals think that people who suffer from symptoms such as mine aren't human? I explained to them that I don't eat pork or beef, but I wasn't given an option. I barely ate anything in a hospital, because there was so much pork and beef but very few vegetables and fruits.

Among several other uncomfortable side effects, I suffered from involuntary muscle movement for two weeks before I was offered a shot of Benadryl. Let me tell you—involuntary muscle movement hurts like hell! It felt weird to be with other people and suddenly find myself unable to control the entire right side of my body. My muscles from head to toe would tense up painfully—eyes, arms, mouth, and so on.

I often thought, *Why doesn't anyone think about the feelings or the dignity of mentally ill people?* Usually I don't believe in the term *mental illness*, but I'm using it here because it's universally understood. Being in the hospital made me feel like less of a person because my rights were taken from me. I wasn't fed adequately, my right to choose for myself was gone, and I suffered from several side effects. How was that helping me? It just made my symptoms worse, and I started to get depressed.

Over the years, I have learned to distinguish between good and bad entities. I recognize how I feel when they appear. When I'm calm, I know it's a good entity, so I let it be or ignore it. When it's a bad entity—or rather, a *dark* entity—my impulse is to run and hide.

These entities *want* me to *see* them, but they stay too far away for me to touch them.

BRAIN WAVE OF THOUGHT

Working in the mental health field, I have noticed a huge separation between the various disciplines. The social worker is thought to sit on the pedestal, even in the eyes of clinical assessment and billing, but we also have mental health counselors, psychologists, marriage and family therapists, and addiction therapists. I have personally witnessed people having more than one clinician on their schedule, especially when child protective services is involved, but none of those clinicians talk to one another. Prescribing doctors don't ask therapists about mental health progress so that they can accurately determine if the medication is working. Therapists see their clients once or twice a week and hear about their most intimate moments, and yet … Well, in my experience, I have never received, from the individual responsible for medication management, a release for my clinical assessment of a client.

I point this out because in my own experience, I was left to take medication without any follow-up. My numbing experiences as a hospital inpatient have traumatized me to this day. Now I feel a personal responsibility to attempt to involve myself in all aspects of my clients' lives by creating care teams for them. Although I haven't been too successful, I try to advocate for adequate care that involves everyone: nutritionist (for addiction counseling), medical doctor, prescribing medical doctor, and so on.

Clinicians should also have a policy regarding follow-ups. My inpatient experiences only validated my thoughts of loneliness and abandonment. I put my trust in the mental health experts so that I could be a productive citizen, but in my opinion I was treated like a prisoner. We have to walk what we preach. We can't think that our duty is limited to a sixty- to ninety-minute session. Further advocacy for adequate treatment is needed. I have had several opportunities to go to Washington and fight for more money for mental health treatment, but I ignore them. Why? I can't see myself fighting for more money when most mental health therapists and institutions look at their field as a job, rather than genuinely caring about positive change and helping promote wellness. They're not all like that, but the majority are. I have been in several institutions in various cities and states, and they have all validated my view thus far.

I don't mean to sway clients away from seeking help. There are some great therapists out there, and there's revolutionary research on how to prevent experiences like mine from happening again. I also hope that this book will promote change and encourage counseling interns to be mindful and competent in engaging with clients. If only one person is moved, I will be satisfied in my mission.

DISRUPTION OF FAMILY BY SEPARATION OR DIVORCE

DURING MY TEENAGE YEARS, I BECAME CONFUSED ABOUT MY sexuality. One day I went with my sister's father to the home of one of his nieces. While she and I were alone in the house, she asked me to dance with her. I didn't think anything of it, so I got up and danced with her. It was a slow song, and as we danced, she started kissing my neck. I didn't know what she was doing. As I mentioned earlier, my childhood did not involve being sexual or wanting to be in a relationship. She would kiss me and ask me to touch her. I might have been around ten years old. I never thought too much of those interactions with her, although it happened every time I went to her house.

I don't remember when it started, but I began having dreams about sexual encounters with women. In my dreams, I couldn't make out their faces and I never reached a climax, but I would wake up aroused. This happened for several years, and I eventually concluded that I liked women. So I planned to live my life as a lesbian and date only women, but apparently the universe saw otherwise and I continued to have nonsexual relationships with men. Believe me—I tried to be in a same-sex relationship, but it never seemed to work. In fact, I met my first husband when I was fifteen years old.

I had seen him here and there on the block of Lafayette, although I didn't have any personal contact with him. But then one day a film producer came to our block to cast some children for his movie, and my mother arranged for me to play the lead child in the movie. I played a young girl, in a relationship with a young man, who had a child and went on to experience various struggles. In the movie, my future husband played my boyfriend.

After that, I started to talk to him more. He was a perfect gentleman in every way, and eventually our relationship became sexual. We still have a great relationship today, and I know that I can call on him for anything. One day, sitting on my mother's porch in the middle of the summer, we decided to have a child together. Soon I was a sixteen-year-old girl pregnant with my first son.

My mother didn't agree with our decision, and she tried with her whole soul to get me to get an abortion. Taking me along with her, she asked several people to help her pay for an abortion. Every single person said that I was worthless and that I'd never succeed in life. Several people stamped "dropout" on my forehead—or at least that's what it felt like to me. One person called me a bitch and a whore to my face.

After we visited several people, my mom isolated me in my bedroom. I couldn't come out except to use the bathroom. Eventually she kicked me out of the house, and I went to stay with my uncle. It was nice of him to take me in, but he didn't take care of me the way I felt he should have. I am grateful that he opened his home to me, but as a pregnant teenager who had been kicked out of her mother's home, I could have benefited from someone talking to me. I was living in his house, but we had very little interaction. It was like I was there ... alone, and I had to fend for myself.

My child's father got a job and started giving me money for food, and eventually he rented a place for us to stay together. We lived in that rented basement until I had my son. I was determined to do good for my child. I finished school and got two jobs to support us. When I turned eighteen years old, we got married and had two more children. We stayed together for over ten years, though eventually we grew apart and decided to separate. He complained that I was too focused on school and my career. I would be gone all day at work, and when I finally got home, I'd get straight on my computer to do schoolwork. His frustration was understandable, but I really felt that I had to prove my success to those who had doubted me. Also, he was insecure because he couldn't please me sexually. I tried everything to get myself to climax, but … nothing. I forced myself to have relations with him more often, so that he would be happy and stop worrying about whether I was satisfied. I never asked him about that, so I don't know if my strategy worked.

More importantly, I believe that my marriage failed because of my paranoia and "mental illness." He was with me through all the hallucinations. Night after night, I woke him up because I was in the dark or needed to use the bathroom. I couldn't even walk to the bathroom by myself at night, because I was too scared that something was after me. I spent night after night crying because I felt like I wasn't loved. My first interaction with a man eventually traumatized me. Why? I would never experience sexual pleasure like other people did, and he deserved to be with someone he could make climax. At the end of the day, he was a man—and men want to feel superior, right? Their ego wants to make a woman scream with pleasure, right?

This thinking plagued me for more than ten years. Can you imagine feeling inadequate for that long? How would you feel? What would you do? Not only could my husband not please me sexually, but I was hallucinating and suffering anxiety attacks that were unbearable to *me*. I felt like I was walking on eggshells in my relationship. Every day I worried that he was going to leave me, but I didn't know what I was doing. I never was loved … or was I? Even now I don't know love, though I am learning. As a child, I never experienced trust and security with my family, so how could I do so in my marriage? These things called love, hugs, and affection remained foreign to me, even though he tried to give them to me every day. He was a perfect man.

Here I am mentally creating situations to make sense of my unrealistic thoughts. I would sit around thinking that he didn't love me. How could he, when no one else did? Why should I stay faithful? Why should I give him my all? Just so he could manipulate me? Why? As I look back on our time together, I realize that he did *nothing* to make me feel that way. It was just my childhood experiences carried over into adult situations.

If he ever reads this, I hope it helps him understand what I was thinking and going through. I hope he can understand how my "issues" created false realities, which then caused me to act as if things had actually happened that way. I didn't mean to be manic all the time or to always question his love. I loved him! I hope that by explaining what was going on in my mind, I can help others in similar situations to see how it was *in my mind*. Nothing was real except the love that my husband had for me, but my mind wouldn't allow it to come through as such.

Because of my own baggage and insecurities, I created a reality that never actually existed. When people have relationship problems, they need to reflect on themselves. If I had known then what I know now, I would still be married to that man. I have no regrets—only experiences. My experiences caused me to feel insecure. My experiences made me believe that I was unlovable, and then kept me from accepting love from others. My experiences caused me to create realities that did not exist, which hindered my marriage. My experiences caused me to reflect on my past and want to love. My experiences caused me to change my reality—to remarry and know love for a second time. My experience allowed me to recognize real love this time around and appreciate it. My experiences wrote this manuscript.

BRAIN WAVE OF THOUGHT

Think about my previous brain wave of thought. Clinicians, do you see a trend? Take a break from reading and do some mindful breathing. The next chapter will be overwhelming for many people, so let's do a breathing technique:

- Exhale completely through your mouth, making a *whoosh* sound.
- Close your mouth and inhale quietly through your nose to a mental count of four.
- Hold your breath for a count of seven.
- Exhale completely through your mouth, making a *whoosh* sound to a count of eight.
- This is one breath.

ADJUSTMENT DISORDER WITH MIXED DISTURBANCE OF EMOTION AND CONDUCT

OVER THE YEARS, I WATCHED OVER AND OVER AGAIN AS MY MOTHER became quite ill and then improved. She had a bad incident while I was in the military, stationed in Texas, and pregnant with my second child. I was warned over the phone that she might not make it, but when I told my officers, they wouldn't let me take a leave. One officer even made fun of the situation. I didn't understand why they wouldn't let me leave when I had time on the books for a vacation. Things spiraled out of control, resulting in my first hospitalization and a discharge from the military. When I found out that I had been discharged, I got in my car and drove nonstop from Texas to my home in Chicago. I needed to get to my mother as fast as possible.

She did eventually get better, but this cycle of my mother getting sick and then getting better continued for years. I set aside money for her, and I would take her to run errands when I was available. I washed my clothes at her house just to spend time with her. She showed me the insurance plans she had bought for her children and grandkids. She loved my cooking, especially my greens and lasagna. She was an amazing woman who did anything she could to help out anyone who needed it.

One day she came to my house to spend the night, bringing her medication, clothes, and other personal items with her. When she and my husband left to go to the store, curiosity flooded me. Opening her bag, I grabbed a few prescription bottles to see what she was really taking. I looked up the name of one medication ... and then a second name, and a third. Then I sat back in my chair in disbelief, thinking that life as I knew it had just ended. My mother had HIV. I quickly put her medication back in her bag and quietly sat in my room. I didn't know what emotion I should be feeling as I sat there putting everything together. All the hospital visits, long absences, sick days, and blank stares—everything made sense. I pulled myself together and started cooking and listening to music, so that I would be okay when she and my husband got back from the store.

After that, I was very careful with her. I also offered to move my whole family to Texas, so that she could stay with me and avoid the harsh Chicago winters, but she didn't want to do that. Every time she got sick, I worried that it would be the last time. For years, my heart would drop with every cough, every fever, every "Oh, my stomach hurts." I went to her house just to play cards or watch a movie. And yes, I would still climb into my mother's bed and fall asleep across her legs. I never spoke with her—or anyone else—about what I knew. I figured she would tell me when she was ready, or maybe she was embarrassed about it. I would never know.

One day my mother called to tell me that her aunt, who was getting a divorce and going through tough times, was moving in with her. That aunt had stayed with my mother for a while in their younger years, and my mother had always told us that she could tell her aunt anything. Then things started to get weird at my mother's home. She was healthy for a long time, but then one day she wasn't feeling well. She wanted to go to the emergency room, so my little sister took her to Jackson Park Hospital. When my mother went through the admission process, she listed her aunt as the emergency contact. I went to visit my mother in the hospital, and she was sitting up and joking around with me. She even told me that she couldn't wait to be released because she wanted an Italian beef sandwich. I finished my visit and left to go home.

Two days later, I got the call. My mother was on life support. *What?* Rather than immediately rushing to the hospital, I quietly sat in my room for a while to process things. When I got to the hospital, my mother was in ICU on life support. She was awake, but she couldn't talk because of a tube in her throat. I asked my mother's aunt what had happened, but she wasn't clear with me. Nor would the doctors disclose anything to me, because my mother had signed a form authorizing her aunt to make all decisions for her. That was confusing, but okay.

When my mother saw me, she tried to tell me something, but I couldn't make out what she was saying. Then she started crying, which I couldn't bear to watch. I immediately left the room, but then my husband told me that she was trying to tell me not to leave. So I went back into her room and stayed as long as I could without panicking. After she went to sleep, I left. The next day they said that she was doing great and they were going to send her to a facility to recuperate. She just needed to stay in ICU for a few more days until her levels normalized without the monitor support.

A couple of days later, I got another call to go to the hospital. When I got there, I was told that my mother's heart had stopped. Someone had given her an unauthorized shot to the heart, and they had been doing CPR on her for thirty minutes. After what seemed like an eternity, the doctors gathered us in a room and everyone around me started crying. We sat in that room for a long time. I didn't know what was going on, and my aunt and uncles kept looking at me. I was just calmly waiting for the doctors to say that although she had given them a scare, she was going to be okay.

The doctor finally arrived. Apparently my mother's heart had stopped, and by the time they got it beating again, she was brain dead because of a lack of oxygen. At that point, according to the doctor, her heart was the only organ that hadn't failed. She was unable to hear, see, or feel anything. I continued to sit there quietly while everyone around me broke down. When the doctor asked what to do next, I calmly told him to pull the plug—which infuriated my siblings and the rest of my family. But I knew that the rational thing to do was to let my mother rest, so that she would no longer have to suffer with the aches and pains of that disease.

I felt that everyone else was being selfish. I was the one who made sure her bills got paid and her heat stayed on. I furnished her home so she wouldn't be sleeping on the cold floor. I was there from the beginning, sacrificing my career—my life—to take care of my mother. Even now, I don't think my siblings know that the money for their clothes and the other things they needed came from me. My mother couldn't afford to help them, because her Social Security check was so small. How could they be so selfish? Why would they want her to continue living in misery for them? They made me so angry.

We left that waiting room and walked back to my mother's room, where we gathered around her, prayed, and said our final goodbyes. When I reached down to touch her, she was ice cold. I looked over and saw a hand reach from the other side of the curtain to turn the monitor off. The whole room went dark as the cries got louder and the prayers more intense. We stood there and watched my mother's heart monitor. She stayed strong for a while, but about two hours later the monitor's beeping began to slow down.

At this point, I broke down. Was this it? Was this my new reality? I got angry. How dare she leave me without *ever* giving me a hug? How dare she leave without *ever* telling me that she loved me, or that she was proud of me? *How fucking dare that woman just leave me like that?* I took my time giving her a hug, because this time she couldn't push me away. Not this time ... Would this be the first and last hug I would ever experience with my mother?

I stood there for what seemed like an eternity while that monitor beeped ten times, nine, eight, seven, six, five, four, three, two ... One final beep, and then she flatlined and was gone. My heart, my love, my only and everything, was gone. Whose legs was I supposed to lie on now? Whom was I supposed to call and talk to? Those questions have yet to be answered.

The family walked from the hospital back to my mother's house. I immediately went in her room to look for the insurance policies, but her room was a mess. The only person at home was my mother's aunt, so I asked her what had happened. She told me that she had gone into my mother's room. When I asked why, she said that she had thrown away my mother's medications. I asked why she had done that, but she wouldn't answer me. Then I looked in the place where my mother had kept all her important documents. The life insurance policies for her kids and grandchildren were there, but not her own policy. I panicked. I had personally taken my mother to pay on those policies every month, so I knew she had one. I got angry and lashed out at my mother's aunt, who everyone knew was the beneficiary of my mother's policy. I was hysterical, so my family walked me outside.

I immediately started wondering if my mother's aunt had sabotaged her. My mother had been doing fine, but suddenly her medication was gone and her insurance policy was missing. The family stayed at my mother's house, but I couldn't take it so I went home to think things through. At this point, if we couldn't find the policy, that left me to pay for my mother's funeral.

The next day I went to the hospital to claim possession of the body, and a counselor was called downstairs to talk to me. She told me she had spoken with my mother on her second day of admission. My mother hadn't wanted her kids to oversee any arrangements, because she felt we wouldn't be of sound mind. She also told me that my mother had been HIV positive for eighteen years. She had been waiting for her youngest child to come of age, but she finally couldn't take the suffering anymore.

My mother passed in January 2012. I can't recall the date—I can barely recall the year. I was told by several sources that we could sue the hospital, and my sister hired a lawyer. I dismissed myself from that process, however, because I wasn't ready to face reality. Even now, I believe that I have yet to deal with it. I have spontaneous moments of uncontrollable crying, and I immediately throw it into the back of my mind.

The family fell apart when everyone started arguing about burial plans. (For reasons of confidentiality and my family's privacy, I won't get into specifics.) I wanted her cremated so that I could put her ashes in a pendant and wear it forever. But my siblings wanted her buried, so I decided to agree with their wishes. The funeral was packed, with people in the waiting area, lobby, and outside waiting their turn to come in to see her. My mother, everyone's favorite, had been loved by many.

RANDOM RANT IN THE MOMENT OF ANXIETY

I wrote this chapter in a moment of anxiety and psychosis. I wanted to write authentically about how I think while I'm going through an "episode." Please excuse any discomfort caused by my word choices and thought process. I hope to relate to my readers and provoke thought in clinicians. Take and process it from your own understanding.

IN 2015, I SAW TWO DISTINCT ENTITIES. IT WAS LATE AT NIGHT— almost morning—and I was leaving for work. My husband and I lived at the back of a two-story apartment complex in Indianapolis, Indiana. We resided on the first floor, and there was a family living above us. I walked out to my car and got in, turned my music on to wake myself up, and adjusted my seating. (When my husband drives my car, he changes the settings to suit himself—which irritates me, but in a funny way.) My car was facing the building. As I backed out of the parking spot, I looked up and saw two entities in the upstairs window, which was wide open. They looked like two people fully clothed in winter wear, standing side by side. The light was on behind them, and they were looking down at me ... just staring at me. Their faces looked as if they were twisted.

Following my first instinct, I jumped out of my car, leaving it in the middle of the street. Screaming, I ran to my door and started banging on it. The entities watched me get out of my car and run to the door. But then I was directly under that window, so I couldn't see them and they couldn't see me. My husband opened the door and asked me what was wrong. Hysterically, I told him what I had seen. He walked me outside, and I pointed up to the window— where the blinds were pulled down and the lights were off. It was unbelievable. I had seen those two entities in that window as clearly as I've ever seen anything. I can describe them so exactly that it's as if I dressed them myself. It wasn't unusual for me to see things, but they had always been in a black shadow—never in full form, in color, and watching me like that. If I hadn't seen their faces, I would have thought they were ordinary people. That episode haunted me in many ways. It was not my first time seeing things, of course, but it was the first time I saw something in full flesh.

A few nights later I was asleep in my bed and something woke me up. As I looked toward the master bathroom, which opens off my bedroom, I saw veins coming from the top of the door. They continued to grow upward and onto the wall as I watched for several minutes. I even sat up to make sure I was awake, and the veins continued to grow. The veins didn't scare me, so I eventually looked away and went back to sleep.

A few days later I awoke to start my day, found some clothes to wear, and jumped into the shower. While in the shower, I saw a shadow through the shower curtain, which was semitransparent. I thought it was my husband coming in to use the bathroom. I started talking to him, though I can't really remember what I was talking about. When I turned back to look at the shadow, it wasn't moving. I reached to open the curtain and the shadow immediately jumped at me through the shower curtain. I tried to pull the curtain back and flee, but I couldn't move. I started slowly falling, as if my body were paralyzed. As I fell, I looked around and saw my body slowly moving toward the ground. I moved closer and closer, very slowly downward. Then, out of nowhere, I found myself back in my room and slowly moving back into the position in which I had been sleeping before I woke up.

I lay there in shock ... What had just happened? I had read about out-of-body experiences. Had I just experienced one? I had been in the bathroom, but then I appeared back in my room, slowly lying down in my bed just as I had been before I woke up earlier. I did not look down to see if I was going back into my body. I just let it play out and continued to look in the direction my body was turning. If it was an out-of-body experience, what was the shadow that jumped at me? I have yet to answer that question.

I have lived my life in almost daily fear. Every day I see or hear something. I experience elevated levels of anxiety and insomnia. I fear going to sleep at night because I think something will get me. There are moments of relief, and my husband performs several rituals every night to help me sleep. All doors around me need to be closed, because when doors are cracked open, I sometimes see them open or someone standing on the other side of them. I also need any mirrors or objects that have a reflection to be turned away from me. I believe that mirrors are a gateway to the spirit world. I'm not clear if spirits and entities can come through a mirror, but I do know they can watch us through them.

I do not believe in my diagnosis. I believe that what I see and hear is real. There were several incidents that sealed my conclusion, although if I explained them all, I would never have a completed book for you to read because something else happens every day. I want people to understand that I am not crazy. We are not crazy. Just understand that we see what we see. Denying or making fun of those situations only makes things worse. My husband never denies any situation—he just makes sure that I am safe, the way I ask him to make me safe, and then we move on. It's that simple. Listen to us and keep us safe the way we ask to be made safe—not the way that makes *you* comfortable.

We want to have productive lives, just like you do. Do you think we want to walk around paranoid or afraid all the time? We have a never-ending—*never-ending!*—horror movie playing in our heads. As much as I use my coping skills, to this day I may run up the stairs to my room or hear something coming from behind me. I may wake up and be scared to go to the bathroom. It isn't fun to live with a heightened sense of fear or anxiety all the time.

I've attempted suicide several times in my life—not because I was depressed, but because I didn't understand what I was going through. I had exhausted all avenues of help and still wasn't successfully dealing with everyday life stressors. Medication only sedated me, and therapists never asked useful questions or engaged me in any in-depth conversation. There is no cure for my experiences, and the more I talk about it or attempt to find answers, the worse it can get.

CHILD SEXUAL ABUSE, CONFIRMED, INITIAL ENCOUNTER

At times, I believed I had PTSD as a result of being taken advantage of when I was fourteen years old. It was December, and somewhere—I can't remember where—I met an older guy. He gave me his number and we talked a few times. I didn't know how old he was at the time. One day he asked if we could hang out, so I said sure. But then he said that he wanted to hang out while school was in session, and I really had to think about that. I didn't like to miss school, I told him no.

The next day I saw his car parked on the street about a block from my school. I walked past the car at first, but then I heard him call my name. When I looked back, he was getting out of the car. I walked toward him and asked what he was doing at my school. I remembered that I had told him what school I went to and what time I had to be there. He said that he desperately needed to talk to me, so I said okay but that it had to be quick.

When I got in the car to talk with him, he drove off. I sat there silently, not knowing what was going on. My mother sheltered me when I was a kid, so I had never been in that situation and didn't know what to do. I kept quiet for a few blocks, but finally I asked him what he was doing. He said he had a surprise for me, but that he had forgotten to bring it. He wanted to go home and get it, and then he would take me back to school. We soon arrived at what I believed to be his home. He said that he had bought a pair of Jordans for me, and that he'd prefer for me to try them on upstairs. Then if they didn't fit, he would exchange them and give them to me after school. I said okay.

I went upstairs, where he had left the pair of shoes sitting on a table. I sat down and we talked for a while. He told me how old he was and that he would give me the shoes only if I had sex with him. Then he pulled out a gun, and although he didn't actually point it at me, I immediately feared for my life. So I agreed to have sex with him. The whole time he held me down to penetrate me, I was trying to think of ways to escape. He showed me no mercy, and it was so painful that I cried the whole time. But he didn't care—he just kept going until he was done and then told me to go wash up. I went to the bathroom and saw blood everywhere. What was this? I had never before had sex, so I didn't understand why I was bleeding.

After I washed myself, I heard him go into the bedroom, so I quickly fled his apartment. It was a cold December, and the stairs were slippery with ice buildup. I ran a few blocks and then waited at a bus stop to catch a bus home. I was on Seventy-Fifth near Western, and I needed to make it home to Ninety-Fifth and Jeffrey. For those of you who don't know Chicago, let me tell you—that meant a few hours of riding on the bus. I stood at the bus stop freezing, with no coat or jacket, and crying for a long time until the bus came. I wondered why nobody stopped to ask if I was okay. It was snowing, and a teenager was standing outside in the middle of the day without a coat. I had left my coat, jacket, gloves, scarf, and book bag in the house with him.

I finally made it home and went straight to the bathroom to shower and change clothes. Nobody ever bothered to ask me where my coat was or why I was home early, even though my grandmother, mother, uncle, and uncle's girlfriend were all there. Days went by, and no one seemed to notice that I was going to school with no coat or book bag. I was freezing, but I was also determined to go to school, so I just layered myself with jackets and sweaters.

I felt like it was all my fault. I should never have gotten in that man's car, but how was I to know that something like that might happen? Mom never taught me that there was danger in the world. You may find that hard to believe, especially since we lived in Chicago. Well, although I lived in the heart of the ghetto, I was never outside to experience danger. The people my mother brought into our world were nice, so I tended to trust people. I might have withheld information from them, just because I didn't want everyone knowing my business, but I never doubted that they would fight for me if I needed them.

After about a month, it dawned on me that nobody cared about me. How could they? They never asked me why I didn't have a coat or a book bag. They didn't notice how I had changed. I started to doubt myself, spend a lot of time alone, and generally believe the world to be useless. How could my family not see the difference? How could they not notice that I didn't have a coat? I never told anyone what had happened, because I didn't think it was a big deal. I heard of other people's experiences, and I thought that I had gotten off easy compared with some of them. Later in life, I came to terms with the fact that it hadn't been my fault. I had been manipulated by an older, wiser person who took advantage of a kid. Any child would see a gun and panic, freeze, or fight. I had just wanted to survive.

This incident continues to bother me. To this day, I don't feel any sensation in my personal area, I can't get aroused or climax, and I have moments of crying during and after sex. I'm insecure, and I still believe that the person I'm with will someday leave me because he thinks he can't satisfy me or that I'm just not interested in sex. I've been to a doctor several times, but their routine response is

"Maybe you should try this or that." I've tried all their suggestions, but nothing changes. I was depressed about it for a long time, and I still think about it every now and then. Sometimes I still slip into suicidal ideation, thinking that since no one has ever cared about me, why should I continue living? I have a saying: "If I didn't have kids, I would kill myself right now." Right now, as I write those words, I believe them. I use my children as my motivation to continue in this life.

I have yet to find any internal motivation. How could I? Look around, and all you see is sex depicted in the media. I can't watch a child's cartoon without seeing them popping their butts or a child's movie without a death scene in it. I am reminded of my status and history as an African American. Hip-hop degrades women with bitch this, bitch that, kill you, drug that. In entertainment by other races, they do not use this kind of language or degrade their people. Right now, in 2016, the Black Lives Matter movement has arisen in response to police brutality against blacks. I fear for my children every day when they do not make it home at the expected time, even though right now I live in a predominantly white neighborhood in Indianapolis.

Every day I see people drive by my house with racial flags on their cars. Every day I see evidence of the poverty, bombing, disease, slavery, and stereotyping of the African American people. Maybe it doesn't affect some people, but I feel it. It's discouraging, and it hurts my heart to see this sickness and suffering.

I've tried several routes to help me cope, including spirituality. After talking with my brother about the Bible and the spirit world, I would immediately get a feeling that a spirit was following me or listening in on our conversation. Watching scary movies just fuels my symptoms, because I apply what I see in the film and it manifests into existence. For example, after watching a movie about spirits being in a mirror, I started to believe and see objects in mirrors. Once I begin to see and feel things, I can't convince myself that they don't exist. Sometimes I'll see a trailer for a scary movie, and I think that I'd love to see the film, but I don't because I know what would happen afterward. I try to stay away from certain spiritual conversation or movies with supernatural plots. I love scary movies and find them very entertaining, but I must be careful and mindful of my sanity.

I have found alternative ways to cope with my symptoms. When I have anxiety, for example, I do something productive that requires quick movement, such as exercising, playing with my children, or cleaning up. Music helps as well, because I'm able to focus on it. When I have insomnia, I read a book or finish some schoolwork. I will also agree to work overnight shifts.

Believe it or not, for two years I worked at the same inpatient hospital to which I had been admitted years earlier. Everyone with whom I worked had been there when I was admitted, but I don't think they remembered me. Clients rotate in and out of those places weekly. Unfortunately, I can remember every face I come across. I might not remember your name, but I will remember your face and where you were from.

I recall being treated cruelly by some of these employees, just as they were rude to patients years later while I was employed there. I never said anything, but I made sure to treat all patients with respect and dignity. Based on my own inpatient experience, I believe that everyone is just one nerve away from having a mental breakdown, one incident away from becoming disabled. Every human being should be treated with the same respect, regardless of their circumstances or situation. To this day, I have those employees' phone numbers, and I'm friends with them on Facebook. Maybe after reading this book, they will remember me as a patient, understand what I'm talking about, and change their ways—or maybe that's just wishful thinking.

I tried to find jobs that were flexible and didn't require a typical nine-to-five commitment. For example, I would do contract work where I could schedule myself on a day-by-day basis when I was mentally stable. Then I moved to Indianapolis and opened a social service agency that currently holds three major contracts with the state of Indiana. I own two properties, and I'm now establishing a home health agency. I hold a license and certifications in several areas of community development, counseling, and addiction. I have

THE PATH TO ENLIGHTENMENT

remarried, and we have six children total. I have been nominated for several accolades for my work as a mental health and addiction counselor.

I say all of this to demonstrate that everyone, regardless of their experiences or diagnosis, can have a happy, productive, meaningful life. Looking through the dual lenses of former client and current health care provider, I have come to two conclusions. First, we are all in need of a voice and choice, respect, dignity, and understanding. And second, everyone is just one experience or nerve away from becoming one of the people we serve.

SPECIFIC LEARNING DISORDER, PSYCHOTIC DISORDER

MY PURPOSE IN THIS BOOK IS NOT TO TELL THE MAGNIFICENT STORY of my life but to motivate my readers. I want to inspire people who feel they are nothing more than a product of their environment, to touch the hearts of those who are suffering from mental illness and inspire them to be greater than their diagnosis. My desire is to help caretakers and service providers understand what we are going through and to make them think about how they service the "mentally ill."

In this chapter, I provide information about a few things that readers might not understand. This literature review will define psychotic disorders, emphasize the diagnostic criteria for schizophrenia, and look at how the treatment of psychotic disorders has evolved over the years. I use the *Diagnostic and Statistical Manual of Mental Disorders 4* because the new fifth edition doesn't differentiate between various types of schizophrenia. As I've mentioned previously, I don't believe in a diagnosis of schizophrenia, but it is useful and quite important to know what society has believed schizophrenia to be, how it was treated in the past, and how treatment is attempted today.

HISTORY OF SCHIZOPHRENIA

Psychotic symptoms have been around for centuries, but those who studied them didn't know how to analyze these uncommon behaviors. The specific psychotic symptoms associated with schizophrenia were not identified until a German psychiatrist, Dr. Emil Kraepelin, noticed that schizophrenia had unique features that differentiated it from other mental illnesses (Warner 2004, 4). He identified a specific combination of symptoms that present themselves in early adulthood, including hallucinations, delusions, thought disorders (loose association, incoherence), and varied emotional affects (Warner 2004, 6). Then Kraepelin compared dementias characteristic of declined mental functioning with his observations. That process led him to formulate the term *dementia praecox*, meaning "dementia of early age," to identify schizophrenic symptoms and patients (Medical Research Council 2014).

In the early twentieth century, Eugen Bleuler, a Swiss psychiatrist, noticed that people who received a diagnosis of dementia praecox were starting to recover. Observing patients with this diagnosis, he speculated that they hadn't experienced a mental decline, but instead a lack of association between thought and emotion. He then changed the name of the disorder from dementia praecox, which was misleading, to schizophrenia, meaning "split mind" (Medical Research Council 2014; Werner 2004, 8).

TREATMENTS

Schizophrenia symptoms were an anomalous experience that occurred through intense spiritual emergences, which were viewed as positive experiences. According to Phillips, Lukoff, and Stone (2009), individuals who experienced visions and heard voices were perceived as shamans, prophets, saints, and visionaries.

Over time, specific beliefs have arisen surrounding individuals who experienced visions and voices. Some have believed mental illness to be a result of spiritual and/or demonic possession (Foerschner 2010)—a belief that sparked a lot of barbaric treatment. One early school of thought was to create a place that would help rid an individual of these evil spirits. Facilities were created, staffed with members of the clergy, to assist the individual in ridding themselves of evil spirits by seeking refuge in religion.

ASYLUMS

As those early facilities proved unable to accommodate the growing number of patients, around the sixteenth century, asylums were built. These facilities were known for having untrained, unqualified, and uneducated staff. Both the employees and the families considered asylums as nothing more than drop-off locations for people suffering from a disorder that nobody understood (Foerschner 2010). Eventually employees begin to explore ways to treat patients suffering from mental disturbances, and a wide range of treatment procedures were developed.

One treatment for schizophrenia was to drill a hole in a patient's skull to release the evil spirit that was believed to be trapped inside (Foerschner 2010). By creating a hole in the skull, they could push the spirit out and the patient would not hear voices anymore. Other measures included—but weren't limited to—flogging, starving, bloodletting, castration, and burning patients at the stake. Growing awareness of these cruel, irrational practices created a general stir that resulted in asylum closures and a push toward more ethical treatment of patients suffering from mental illness.

THERAPIES

There have been marked changes in mental health policy regarding how to treat patients suffering from mental illness. In the 1940s, therapeutic concepts and practices sparked a significant change in therapy. In their efforts to define and prove the efficacy of treatment, psychologists and other physicians explored such treatments as insulin therapy, electric shock therapy, and psychosurgery (lobotomies) (Grob 1991, 127).

Insulin therapy. In 1930s, a Viennese physician named Manfred Sakel developed one of the most promising somatic therapies of his time (Grob 1991, 127). He administered large dosages of insulin to patients with schizophrenia to create a hypoglycemic state that helped them sleep. There were claims that this therapy, which was used widely, resulted in effective improvements, at a time when no other interventions seemed to work. However, Sakel's insulin therapy came to be heavily scrutinized because it resulted in a mortality rate of one in five and it wasn't backed up by any conclusive evidence or data (Grob 1991, 127).

Electric shock therapy. Electric shock therapy, now known as electroconvulsive therapy (ECT), was introduced in 1938 by Ug Cerletti and Lucio Bini for the treatment of schizophrenia (Phutane, Thirthalli, and Gangadhar 2011). ECT is a medical procedure that sends electric currents into the brain. It became popular because it was easy to administer and it brought about instant results by changing the brain chemistry (Grob 1991, 128). In 1945, however, the census of patients went up and facilities suffered from a shortage of medical staff. In efforts to maintain control over their patients, the staff began using ECT as punishment, rather than as treatment. High voltages were administered to defiant patients, resulting in memory loss, confusion, and medical complications such as elevated heart rates and blood pressure.

Psychosurgery. Psychosurgery, also known as lobotomy, was pioneered by Egas Moniz in Portugal and first performed in the United States in 1935 by Walter Freeman and James W. Watts (Grob

1991, 129). Moniz reported a 70 percent success rate in controlling compulsions and anxiety in schizophrenic patients, but lobotomies didn't result in concrete results and were irreversible (Grob 1991, 129). This procedure was done by inserting a dull bar through the temples on either side of the head and moving it up and down to destroy brain tissue (Soares et al. 2013).

Lobotomies resulted in calmer patients who exhibited reduced intellectual functioning, an inability to learn, loss of memory, and partial paralysis. There were also reports of confusion, social withdrawal, attention deficits, and—in the most severe cases— epilepsy. Psychosurgery proved to be controversial because it benefited the institutions rather than the patients, who simply became more manageable (Grob 1991, 130). After a lobotomy, patients who had previously exhibited disruptive and unpleasant behaviors became less troublesome (Soares et al. 2013).

Even these treatments were deemed inhumane and cruel, but in the 1950s there was a trend toward administering antipsychotic medications (Lane 2014). This treatment provided more promising results and alleviated the use of extreme, unfounded remedies.

CURRENT PRACTICES

Still today, there exist two distinct beliefs about what schizophrenia is, why it's induced in certain people, and how to treat it. In Western culture, seeing visions and hearing voices has been seen as a psychotic disorder. The general belief is that all genders and ethnic groups are equally at risk, although schizophrenia is rare in children and hard to detect in teenagers. In young people, the illness is considered to be in its prodromal period. Schizophrenia is hard to detect in adolescents because its symptoms mimic typical teenage behavior (National Institute of Mental Health, n.d.). In younger children, early symptoms might include a loss of interest in activities, withdrawal from friends, and a drop of grades.

DIAGNOSING SCHIZOPHRENIA

Schizophrenia is recognized in the *Diagnostic and Statistical Manual of Mental Disorders* (*DSM-4*). To receive a diagnosis of schizophrenia, an individual must have two or more of the following characteristics: delusions (false beliefs), hallucinations (seeing things that no one else can), disorganized speech (such as frequent derailment or incoherence), grossly disorganized or catatonic behavior (episodes of behavior at extreme opposite ends of the spectrum), and negative symptoms such as affective flattening, alogia, or avolition (American Psychiatric Association 1994, 273–315).

The *DSM-4* goes into additional criteria: social/occupational functions (how someone interacts in the environment), duration, schizoaffective and mood disorder (disordered thought process and abnormal emotions) exclusion, substance/general medical condition exclusion, and relationship to a pervasive development disorder (delays in the development of multiple basic functions, including social and communication). The *DSM-4* also recognizes subtypes, which are based on the prominent characteristic of the person at the time (Bengston 2006). Schizophrenic symptoms can progress in different ways over time. As symptoms fluctuate, the subtype of the individual could vary.

Schizophrenia: Paranoid subtype. Schizophrenia paranoid subtype, formerly known as paranoid schizophrenia, is characterized by delusions and auditory hallucinations (Bengston 2006). Individuals with this subtype are usually characterized by normal intellectual functioning and normal affects (Santorelli 2013). The predominant symptoms might include anger, anxiety, and paranoia. According to Bengston (2006), people who have a diagnosis of this subtype tend to be higher functioning than those with other subtypes, and they can appear to live normal lives by managing and learning coping skills. Individuals with this subtype present symptoms in accordance with some characteristic theme that is usually consistent (Bengston 2006). For example, night or darkness could be a trigger for them, or they might believe that someone is out to get them. They will seek medical attention usually when they are experiencing a high level of stress, which escalates the symptoms of paranoia.

Schizophrenia: Catatonic subtype. Catatonic subtype schizophrenia is characterized by disturbances and extreme behaviors on both sides of the spectrum (Santorelli 2013). At one point the individual might display rapid speech, extreme movements, and an inability to sit down. Alternatively, the individual may have extreme low points during which they appear to not move at all, show no interest in activities, and remain speechless for hours (Bengston 2006).

Schizophrenia: Disorganized subtype. This subtype is characterized by disorganized thoughts, speech, and behaviors (Santorelli 2013). These individuals might also exhibit inappropriate, unstable, and/or exaggerated emotional responses, such as laughing hysterically at a funeral. Individuals with this subtype diagnosis might have difficulties communicating effectively, showering, dressing, and caring for themselves in any way (Bengston 2006).

Schizophrenia: Undifferentiated subtype. The undifferentiated subtype is characterized by having a mix of symptoms from the paranoid, disorganized, and catatonic subtypes, but not enough for a specific diagnosis (American Psychiatric Association 1994, 289).

Schizophrenia: Residual subtype. The residual subtype is characterized by having acute to absence of delusions, hallucinations, disorganized speech, and catatonic behavior (American Psychiatric Association 1994, 289). The patient no longer displays severe symptoms, but their symptoms may manifest acutely (Bengston 2006). The person might not present with positive symptoms, but may experience negative symptoms from time to time.

Other associated features might appear and need to be considered when treating people who suffer from schizophrenia. These features include learning disability; hyperactivity; psychosis; euphoric or depressed mood; somatic or sexual dysfunction; guilt or obsession; sexually deviant behavior; odd, eccentric, or suspicious personality; anxious, fearful, or dependent personality; and dramatic, erratic, or antisocial personality (American Psychiatric Association 1994, 273–315).

The other view of schizophrenia is linked closely to older, more traditional beliefs about spiritual experience. To better understand this concept, we must view *spirituality* as distinct from *religion*. For our purposes here, *religion* refers to an organized social group that focuses on human transcendence through believing in a higher power, rituals, and specified doctrine. *Spirituality* refers to the transcendence within one's self to reach full human potential. The focus is on the spiritual experience itself, which might have a connection to schizophrenia. Some clinicians and theorists believe that people who experience spiritual and psychological breaks can continue to develop and work through life's natural developments (Phillips, Lukoff, and Stone 2009).

HOLISTIC TREATMENT

The holistic approach to understanding and treating people with mental health difficulties has paved the way for researchers to examine alternative treatments for sufferers of schizophrenia (Shah, Kulhara, Grover, Kumar, Malhotra, and Tyagi 2011). Since schizophrenia was classified as a mental illness, treatment has remained limited to counseling, institutionalization, and antipsychotic medication (Scholes and Martin 2010). Over the years, however, some people have considered cognitive behavioral therapy to be one of the most effective interventions for people suffering from this disorder.

Holistically, schizophrenia is viewed as an opportunity to grow and explore human potential—a temporary psychotic phase that could initiate change and usefulness (Phillips, Lukoff, and Stone 2009). Coping is defined as a behavioral and cognitive effort to manage one's internal and external responses to environment (Shah et al. 2011). Developing coping skills and integrating spirituality into the treatment process could help reduce the occurrence of symptoms. Coping has been a key focus of care, and this alternative has been explored through several studies.

Research has led to the understanding that coping skills are an effective way to manage schizophrenic symptoms (Lysaker, Tsai, Hammoud, and Davis 2007). Several cross-sectional and longitudinal studies have highlighted the effectiveness of coping skills. A cross-sectional study using the Positive and Negative Syndrome Scale (PANSS) found the personal belief system to be associated with active and adaptive coping skills in subjects with residual schizophrenia (Shah et al. 2011). Similarly, a longitudinal study with a sample of forty-eight young adults found religious coping skills beneficial in developing personal growth and finding spiritual meaning in their diagnosis (Phillips and Stein 2007).

COPING-SKILL APPROACHES

Data has suggested that individuals with schizophrenia disorder may have endured difficulties with managing their symptoms because of maladaptive styles of coping (Lysaker, Tsai, Hammoud, and Davis 2007). The use of coping skills and strategies has been associated with minimizing positive and negative symptoms (MacAulay and Cohen 2013). There are three major approaches to how an individual suffering from schizophrenia looks at coping: self-directing, deferring, and collaborative (Shah et al. 2011).

Self-directed approach. The self-directed approach is when the person is at the center of—and takes an active role in—their own decision making (Pargament, Kennell, Hathaway, Grevengoed, Newman, and Jones 1988). The individual looks within for the answer. They also take responsibility for their decisions and decide what support they need and who will supply that support. An example of the self-directed approach is when the individual looks within himself or herself for the answer, rather than relying on external factors, such as meditating or exercising, to help them manage their symptoms.

Deferring approach. The deferred approach is implied when the individual places their hope for improvement on medication or some other outside force (Shah et al. 2011). The individual believes that someone or something else will make things better for them. An example of the deferred style is implied when the individual puts their hope for improvement on their prescribed medication. They believe they will get better if they will just take their medication.

Collaborative approach. The collaborative approach is like a counseling session in which the individual shares and reflects on their problem-solving ideas and goals, so that their counselor can help guide them through managing their symptoms. The collaborative approach involves an active exchange between the individual and the person whom they trust to assist them (Pargament et al. 1988).

Coping skills and strategies also help this population with social cognition. One of the symptoms of schizophrenia is social withdrawal. Individuals in this population report difficulties in expressing and perceiving emotions (Harvey and Penn 2010). They report feeling uncomfortable or confused about how people perceive them and what they are communicating, and they often display other related symptoms such as paranoia and suspiciousness. Coping strategies such as the collaborative approach help individuals see their irrational thoughts and behaviors about other people and better understand the reality of their relationships with other people.

SPIRITUAL AND RELIGIOUS APPROACH

Anton Boisen, the founder of pastoral counseling, recognized that people who suffer from schizophrenia may experience delay in the development of their spiritual selves (Phillips, Lukoff, and Stone 2009). This delay creates spiritual issues that mimic schizophrenic symptomology. Boisen believed that the therapist should not hinder the process but instead help guide the client in unfolding and finding ways to face the situations that are causing the distress. Boisen believed that there is a natural problem-solving method in coping that helps with spiritual difficulties.

People who suffer from schizophrenia have found that various coping skills have been beneficial in managing distressful symptoms (Shah et al. 2011). The literature supports the argument that an individual's belief system, ranging from spirituality to motivation, influences how they cope. This population has benefited from spiritual and religious ties to counseling that help them develop and strengthen their beliefs in themselves. Religion and spirituality have been known to provide a support system and a source of meaning. In religious settings such as churches or other sacred places, people find refuge, support from other believers, and encouragement and guidance through the sacred doctrines.

Spirituality and other holistic approaches help schizophrenic sufferers by providing meaning in life and a sense of connectedness to other people. Most people who suffer from this disorder feel isolated and distressed, so it is important for them to find ways to reduce their need for isolation and personal control (Shah et al. 2011). Creating a sense of connectedness could help this population with their feelings, thoughts, and relationships, thus promoting a more positive coping experience by providing them with hope and motivation in managing their disorder (Shah et al. 2011). According to Shah et al. (2011), "61–80% of patients with a diagnosis of schizophrenia resort to religion to cope with their symptoms and difficulties." This is an abundance of individuals who have found relief in incorporating and using their coping strategies to combat symptoms.

There are also cultural implications associated with how people look to faith and spirituality for relief of their symptoms. For example, people who consider spirituality as part of their approach to managing their disorder tend to be in the lower socioeconomic strata (Rammohan, Rao, and Subbakrishna 2002). It is speculated that because of their lack of resources, people of lower socioeconomic status will make good use of whatever they have. Faith and spirituality is an effective—and cost-effective—way for this population to focus on reducing their distress and burden by exploring problem-solving coping skills (Rammohan et al. 2002). Using spirituality to cope when there are limited resources has significant outcomes for psychological well-being.

FUTURE RESEARCH

People who suffer from schizophrenia have found that various coping skills have been beneficial in managing distressful symptoms (Shah et al. 2011). Many types of treatment have been applied to schizophrenia in hopes of alleviating symptoms. Some approaches have proven to be effective, although in the past, these approaches often failed to cite empirical data as evidence of their effectiveness. Currently research has provided only minimal evidence of the effective difference between one approach and another.

There has been only minimal advancement in the literature regarding schizophrenia and even less information forthcoming on the effectiveness of one approach over another. Schizophrenia is viewed as an illness that will not go away, so managing schizophrenia— rather than preventing or curing it—has been the focus of treatment. Few researchers have reached sound conclusions in their applications or results. More testing is needed, using a larger sample size and a sturdy methodological foundation. This chapter's literature review has led me to a recognition of the need for further scientific research.

REFERENCES

American Psychiatric Association. 1994. *Diagnostic and Statistical Manual of Mental Disorders* 4th ed. Washington, DC: American Psychiatric Association. doi:http://justines2010blog.files. wordpress.com/2011/03/dsm-iv.pdf.

Bengston, M. 2006. *Types of Schizophrenia*. Retrieved from http:// psychcentral.com/lib/types-of-schizophrenia/000714.

Foerschner, A. M. 2010. "The History of Mental Illness: From 'Skull Drills' to 'Happy Pills.'" *The International Student Journal* 2 (9): 1–4. Retrieved from http://www.studentpulse.com/articles/283/2/ the-history-of-mental-illness-drills-to-happy-pills.

Grob, G. N. 1991. *From Asylums to Community: Mental Health Policy in Modern America*. Princeton, NJ: Princeton University Press.

Harvey, P. D., and D. Penn. 2010. "Social Cognition: The Key Factor Predicting Social Outcome in People with Schizophrenia?" *Psychiatry* 7 (2): 41–44.

Henry, J. D., C. von Hippel, and L. Shapiro. 2010. "Stereotype Threat Contributes to Social Difficulties in People with Schizophrenia." *British Journal of Clinical Psychology* 49 (1): 31–41. doi:10.1348/014466509X421963.

Jones, K. 1993. *Asylums and After: A Revised History of the Mental Health Services: From the Early 18ᵗʰ Century to the 1990s.* London: Athone Press.

Lane, C. 2014. *History of Schizophrenia.* Retrieved from http://www.schizophrenia.com/content/schizophrenia/history-schizophrenia.

Lysaker, P. H., J. Tsai, K. Hammoud, and L. W. Davis. 2009. "Patterns of Coping Preference among Persons with Schizophrenia: Associations with Self-Esteem, Hope, Symptoms and Function." *International Journal of Behavioral Consultation and Therapy* 5 (2): 192–208.

Lysaker, P. H., C. Tunze, P. T. Yanos, D. Roe, J. Ringer, and K. Rand. 2012. "Relationships between Stereotyped Beliefs about Mental Illness, Discrimination Experiences, and Distressed Mood over 1 Year among Persons with Schizophrenia Enrolled in Rehabilitation." *Social Psychiatry and Psychiatric Epidemiology* 47 (6): 849–855. doi:10.1007/s00127-011-0396-2.

MacAulay, R., and A. S. Cohen. 2013. "Affecting Coping: Does Neurocognition Predict Approach and Avoidant Coping Strategies within Schizophrenia Spectrum Disorders?" *Psychiatric Research* 209 (2): 136–141. doi.org/10.1016/j.psychres.2013.04.004.

Martens, W. J. 2010. "Positive Functions of Psychosis." *Journal of Phenomenological Psychology* 41 (2): 216–233. doi:10.1163/156916210X532135.

Martens, W. J. 2012. "Healing Dynamics of Psychosis." *International Forum of Psychoanalysis* 21 (2): 68–81. doi:10.1080/0803706X.2011.592509.

Medical Research Council. 2014. *Achievements and Impact: Schizophrenia.* Retrieved from http://www.mrc.ac.uk/Achievementsimpact/Storiesofimpact/Schizophrenia/index.htm.

Mohr, S., L. Borras, C. Betrisey, B. Pierre-Yves, C. Gilliéron, and P. Huguelet. 2010. "Delusions with Religious Content in Patients with Psychosis: How They Interact with Spiritual Coping."

Psychiatry: Interpersonal and Biological Processes 73 (2): 158–172. doi:10.1521/psyc.2010.73.2.158.

National Institute of Mental Health. n.d. *What Is Schizophrenia?* Retrieved from http://www.nimh.nih.gov/health/topics/schizophrenia/index.shtml#part1.

Pargament, K. I., J. Kennell, W. Hathaway, N. Grevengoed, J. Newman, and W. Jones. 1988. "Religion and the Problem-Solving Process: Three Styles of Coping." *Journal for the Scientific Study of Religion* 27 (1): 90–104. doi:10.2307/1387404.

Phillips, R., and C. H. Stein. 2007. "God's Will, God's Punishment, or God's Limitations? Religious Coping Strategies Reported by Young Adults Living with Serious Mental Illness." *Journal of Clinical Psychology* 63 (6): 528–540. doi:10.1002/jclp.20364.

Phillips, R., D. Lukoff, and M. K. Stone. 2009. "Integrating the Spirit within Psychosis: Alternative Conceptualizations of Psychotic Disorders." *Journal of Transpersonal Psychology* 41 (1): 61–80.

Phutane, V. H., J., Thirthalli, and B. N. Gangadhar. 2011. "Why Do We Prescribe ECT to Schizophrenia Patients?" *Indian Journal of Psychiatry* 53 (2): 149–151. Retrieved from http://www.ncbi.nlm.nih.gov/pmc/articles/PMC3136018/.

Rammohan, A. A., K. Rao, and D. K. Subbakrishna. 2002. "Religious Coping and Psychological Wellbeing in Carers of Relatives with Schizophrenia." *Acta Psychiatrica Scandinavica* 105 (5): 356–362. doi:10.1034/j.1600-0447.2002.1o149.x.

Razaili, S. M., S. Hussein, and T. Ismail. 2010. "Perceived Stigma and Self-Esteem among Patients with Schizophrenia." *International Medical Journal* 17 (4): 255–260.

Read, J., R. Fosse, A. Moskowitz, and B. Perry. 2014. "The Traumagenic Neurodevelopmental Model of Psychosis Revisited." *Neuropsychiatry* 4 (1): 65–79.

Revheim, N., W. M. Greenberg, and L. Citrome. 2010. "Spirituality, Schizophrenia, and State Hospitals: Program Description and Characteristics of Self-Selected Attendees of a Spirituality

Therapeutic Group." *Psychiatric Quarterly* 81 (4): 285–292. doi:10.1007/s11126-010-9137-z.

Saavedra, J. 2011. "Coping with Positive Symptoms and Disruptive Behaviors." *International Journal of Mental Health* 40 (4): 50–63. doi:10.2753/IMH0020-7411400404.

Santorelli, N. 2013, April 26. *Schizophrenia Types and Symptoms.* Retrieved from http://www.webmd.com/schizophrenia/guide/schizophrenia-symptoms?bookmark=true.

Scholes, B., and C. R. Martin. 2010. "Could Repressive Coping Be a Mediating Factor in the Symptom Profile of Individuals Diagnosed with Schizophrenia?" *Journal of Psychiatric and Mental Health Nursing* 17:403–410. doi:10.1111/j.1365-2850.2009.01537.x.

Shah, R., P. Kulhara, S. Grover, S. Kumar, R. Malhotra, and S. Tyagi. 2011. "Relationship between Spirituality/Religiousness and Coping in Patients with Residual Schizophrenia." *Quality of Life Research: An International Journal of Quality of Life Aspects of Treatment, Care, and Rehabilitation* 20 (7): 1053–1060. doi:10.1007/s11136-010-9839-6.

Soares, M. S., W. S. Paiva, E. Z. Guertzenstein, R. L. Amorim, L. S. Bernardo, J. F. Pereira ... M. J. Teixeira. 2013. "Psychosurgery for Schizophrenia: History and Perspectives." *Neuropsychiatric Disease and Treatment* 2013 (9): 509–515. doi.org/10.2147/NDT.S35823.

Warner, R. 2004. *Recovery from Schizophrenia: Psychiatry and Political Economy.* 3rd ed. New York: Brunner-Routledge.

Printed in the United States
By Bookmasters